Schizoaffective: A Happier and Healthier Life

By
Mary Dodds

PublishAmerica
Baltimore

First printing

ISBN: 1-4241-9474-1
PUBLISHED BY PUBLISHAMERICA, LLLP
www.publishamerica.com
Baltimore

Printed in the United States of America

To my beloved husband, who took over caring for me during the times I couldn't
And never complained about it once

Contents

INTRODUCTION

This is not a textbook about schizoaffective disorder. This book is about what you need to do about your diagnosis to stay as happy and as healthy as you can. I describe how I have learned to cope with and even overcome most of the symptoms of schizoaffective disorder during the past fourteen years.

The first thing people asked when I told them I was writing a book about schizoaffective disorder was, "How can someone who has schizoaffective disorder write a book?" My answer is that you can do anything you put your mind to— even if you are mentally ill. It is true that this illness is a difficult one. You can have great days and you definitely will have some bad days. But the great days make the bad days bearable. The harder you fight this illness, the better off you will be.

The next thing they ask is, "You're not cured. You still even go to the hospital sometimes. What could you possibly have to tell me?" How I handle being hospitalized is an example of how this book can help you. Schizoaffective disorder or any serious mental illness can mean that coping with extremely stressful situations is best handled with a brief hospitalization. It's not inevitable, but it's a possibility. The key is to plan ahead. I found out the name of the best psychiatric facility in my area while I was still feeling well. When the time came and the stress became too much for me, I made sure I went to that facility. I also made sure I ended up in a private facility instead of one run by the state.

While I am out of the hospital I have a fantastic counselor and go to the best clinic. I make sure I understand all my medications and when I should take them. I keep track of which medications have given me problems in the past so that I don't have to experience the side effects twice. I have overcome my problems with substance abuse. I am happily married, back working part-time writing, and am well enough to write this book.

This book is about getting your life back and even working again. It is filled with strategies for people who are new to serious mental illness, experienced veterans, or caregivers for someone with bipolar disorder, schizophrenia or schizoaffective disorder. This book contains what I wish someone had told me when I was first diagnosed. I hope you will find this book helpful.

CHAPTER ONE
DIAGNOSIS

I've just been diagnosed with schizoaffective disorder (or bipolar disorder or schizophrenia). Is my life over?

No. As strange as this may sound, this is actually good news. You finally know what the problem is, so this is the beginning of your recovery. You are starting a whole new chapter of your life. And you're not alone. About three percent of the population of the United States suffer from serious mental illness over the course of a year.[1]

I would bet you haven't been feeling very well before you were diagnosed. The diagnosis just means that now you and your doctor know what the problem really is. It means that you can get help and start feeling better.

Should I be afraid now that schizoaffective disorder is in my medical records?

I met a lady online in a group for people with schizoaffective disorder[2] whose doctor had frightened her to death about putting the diagnosis in her medical records. He convinced her it would be a terrible thing if that happened. He had her very scared about her new diagnosis.

I completely disagree with this doctor's attitude. First of all, I've been diagnosed with bipolar with psychotic features or schizoaffective disorder for fourteen years. Nothing bad has happened because these diagnoses were in my records. If your diagnosis is not in your records, how are the doctors going to know how to help you? Your records are private and confidential. You need to be worried about getting better. You don't need to worry about what is in your medical records.

Why me?

There is no answer to this question. You do not have schizoaffective disorder because you did something wrong. You are not ill because of sin. Genetics play a large part in who gets serious mental illness[3].

You didn't choose this. You can't "snap out of it." It's a real, physical, chronic illness[4] that is going to follow you for the rest of your life (just like diabetes). It's not your fault. But it is your responsibility to take care of yourself. You are the only person who can do this. And if you do take care of yourself with the help of other people, such as your doctor and your counselor, you are going to feel a lot better. You can overcome almost all the symptoms if you try very hard.

Who is going to help take care of me?

The truth is you have just been handed a lot of responsibility. You can ask for and receive help from many different people (doctors, nurses, pharmacists, counselors, family, friends, therapy group members, substance abuse specialists, pastors, church members, hospital staff) but you are responsible for asking for help and taking action. No one can really help you until you take responsibility for yourself.

Is it possible I have something other than schizoaffective disorder?

You need to be honest with yourself about something. You may have another problem in addition to mental illness. Approximately twenty-one percent of the American adults living with a serious mental illness had alcohol or substance abuse problems, compared to 7.9 percent of adults without a serious mental illness, according to the 2003 National Survey on Drug Use and Health.[5] Many of the symptoms of continued drug and alcohol abuse can be the same as or worse than the symptoms of serious mental illness![6]

If you have a substance abuse problem you need to tell your doctor or counselor about the problem right now. The doctor cannot diagnose, treat, and properly medicate you until he or she knows about the substance abuse problem. Your medical records are confidential and you are not going to get in any trouble by being honest. Your honesty is crucial if you want to feel better.

I know how difficult it is to tell someone you have this problem. It means you can't keep letting the problem slide on by. Admitting it means you have to get help and stop using. If you are using every day, you may not feel that you can have a happy life beyond substance abuse. I am telling you from experience you can stop using and your life is going to become so much better you will hardly believe it.

Psychiatric medication should be taken only if you really need it. Don't take a lot of psychiatric medicine to mask symptoms of alcohol or substance abuse. Your problems will just get worse and worse.

If you are one of the lucky four out of five who does not have a substance abuse problem, be very careful not to start one. Stay away from alcohol and illegal drugs and the people who abuse them. I don't care how much of a friend you think they are or if they are a member of your family. You have a greater risk of developing a substance abuse problem than most people. It's not worth the risk to spend time with someone who has a substance abuse problem.

If it happens to be someone in your family who has a problem, try not to be alone with them and stay away from them when they are using. Make sure someone who does not have a problem is there with you when you see them. If your friends have substance abuse problems you are just going to have to find new friends. You have to if you want to take care of yourself.

What is the most important thing I can do to feel better?

Sleep. You need to sleep on a regular schedule. Not sleeping can be the first sign that either something is wrong or you are having a manic episode. Lack of sleep can trigger a manic episode.[7] Lack of sleep makes me feel worse and worse the longer it goes on and if I do not get help I end up in the hospital. If I try to drink alcohol to go to sleep after I've been up all night I really get in trouble. Take your medication at the same time every night and try to go to sleep at the same time each night.

You need to be on enough medication to help you sleep regularly. Alcohol every night to go to sleep is very tempting and may make you sleep for now, but is not going to make you feel better in the long run. Tell your doctor if you are using alcohol to get to sleep. Ask for your medication to be adjusted so you can sleep without alcohol. You'll feel a lot better.

CHAPTER TWO
SYMPTOMS

What symptoms will I experience?

The main symptoms people with schizophrenia and schizoaffective disorder experience are hallucinations, delusions, and sometimes paranoia[8]. People with bipolar disorder and schizoaffective disorder experience mania and depression.[9] There are many more symptoms but this book is only about the most common. Schizoaffective.org on the internet has a complete list of symptoms.

Hallucinations and Delusions

An example of a hallucination is seeing a person or thing that really isn't there. An example of a delusion and paranoia is believing that the FBI or CIA is after you or sending you on a special mission. The problem is learning the difference between hallucinations, delusions, paranoia, and reality.

When you are experiencing hallucinations they can seem so real that it is almost impossible to tell it's not really happening. The movie *A Beautiful Mind* demonstrates very well what having hallucinations is like and how a man named John Nash learned to ignore his hallucinations.

Mania and Depression

People with schizoaffective and bipolar disorder have cycles of mania and depression. Mania is a very high, "up" feeling that some people enjoy. They feel like they are on top of the world. Some people spend a lot of money when they feel manic or think they have special abilities or a special purpose. Others have problems with promiscuous sex (a lot of casual sex with a lot of people). It is a very out-of-control feeling for me. But some people's experience with it is completely different from mine. They like it. It makes a lot of people feel they are completely in control of everything.

Some people enjoy feeling manic so much they do not want to take their medication. They stop taking their medicine because they feel so good. A lot of them end up in the hospital. I hate feeling manic because it means I will not be able to go to sleep for days. If I can't get medical help to get to sleep for three or four days, I do end up in the hospital. Stopping your medication is the best way I know of to end up hospitalized.

As high as you may feel when you are manic, you always swing back down low again. This is the depressive phase. Some people cycle down in a few hours, others in a few days. Depression can cause thoughts of death or suicide. This is when you have a higher risk of suicide than most people. If you ever do feel suicidal, tell someone right away and get help.

When I am manic I stay in bed trying to keep things from going out of control. If I get into any stressful situations at all the mania gets worse. I haven't had any problem with it lately. My medication is handling the mania very well. I have only had one manic episode which put me in the hospital in the last two years. Before that I hadn't had a problem with mania in so long that I was not even taking medication to prevent mania.

When I am very depressed I stay in bed also, because it is so hard to get out of bed at all. You can tell exactly how I'm doing by how clean the house is and whether I bother to put on make up in the morning. There are a lot of clues to show you you're going downhill. These signs are different for everyone.

Are you isolated in your house? Are you afraid to answer the phone? Are you eating a lot more or a lot less? These are all signs which can let you know to get help before things get even worse.

CHAPTER THREE
CONTROLLING YOUR SYMPTOMS

How do I get rid of hallucinations and delusions?

There are several techniques people have told me to use to get rid of hallucinations. The first is taking an anti-psychotic medication, such as Seroquel or Geodon. I had more hallucinations when I was on a lower dose of the anti-psychotic I take. The dosage must be high enough to help stop the hallucinations. The dosage must be increased slowly. Be very patient. It may take several visits to the doctor to get the medication right. Too much medication may cause side effects. Too little and the medication doesn't work.

Even when you do achieve the right amount of medication to take, the right amount can change slightly over time. Taking the right medication may not entirely stop the problem. Medications may not completely control your hallucinations or delusions.

What if medication doesn't control all my hallucinations or delusions?

- Reach out and touch them

One technique for getting rid of hallucinations is trying to reach out and touch them. For some people, trying to touch the hallucination makes it go away. This doesn't work for me. I try to touch them and I can't feel them but they don't go away.

- Tell them to stop bothering you

If you are hearing voices, you can speak to the voices either out loud or in your head and simply tell them to go away. You can even yell at them and tell them they are not real. Tell them you don't have time for them. (I wouldn't try this doing this too often in public.)

- Try anything else you can think of

In the film *A Beautiful Mind*, John Nash (who has schizophrenia) swats someone's desk with a newspaper to make his hallucinations be quiet. He then asks the man sitting at the desk, "Could you possibly ignore I just did that?" I know just how he felt. The way you find to control your symptoms can seem very odd to people.

- What hallucinations did you experience?

I almost never have hallucinations any more. I used to hear someone banging on the door at night. There was really no one there. I would wake up my husband and ask him, "Did you hear that?" He has been very patient about telling me my hallucinations aren't real. I hesitate to tell you what my hallucinations are because they are very strange. I see white wispy strings in the air that float around. Sometimes they change into spiders.

How did you get rid of your hallucinations?

- Time of day

I thought about what time of day my hallucinations

showed up. It was always around seven or eight at night until I went to sleep. They were happening when it was dark outside and I was tired. If your hallucinations happen at the same time each day, either sleep during that time period or change whatever it is you do at that time of day.

I adjusted my sleep schedule. I started getting up and getting to work at four or five in the morning and gong to bed before it was dark--before the time the hallucinations started. They have almost completely stopped. Try to think what time of day they start or figure out what is triggering your hallucinations and change your schedule. Change what you are doing.

What else can trigger hallucinations?

- Flashing lights
Flashing lights make me have hallucinations. I figured out that lights shining in my bedroom at night from cars coming down the driveway at our apartment at night was triggering them.

I completely blacked out all the light coming into my bedroom with dark curtains and wood panels. When the flashing lights were stopped the hallucinations stopped.

- Shadows
Some people experience hallucinations from seeing shadows at night. If the shadows at night frighten you, stay inside with the lights on. You need to get creative to stop your hallucinations. Try to figure out what the problem is and solve it. Your counselor and doctor can help you. The answers are different for everyone.

What hallucinations do you still suffer from?

I still hear music playing all the time, every day, in my head. I have learned to ignore it. When I listen to real music that can help. I know this sounds strange, but there are many people in this world who have a soundtrack going in their head they can't stop. They have to learn to ignore it.

Maybe you don't consider yourself recovered if you have a few hallucinations and delusions. But if you can learn to deal with them or ignore them and make as many as possible go away, I think you're a success story.

How do I control mania and depression?

Don't stop taking your medication. I have found that medication stops mania and depression better than anything else. If you feel manic and can't sleep, tell your counselor or doctor as soon as possible. When you feel depressed, do the same thing. The good thing about schizoaffective disorder is that when you are feeling down you can be sure that it won't be too long before you start feeling better. The bad times come in cycles. When you don't feel well, keep telling yourself you know you will feel better soon. It may take days or weeks, but each day you work at it you can feel a little better each day.

How hard should I push myself each day to get better?

At any stage in this illness, you have just so much stress and activity you can handle each day. I can't do as much as I did before I got sick. This might not be true for you. You have to recognize your limitations to keep from suffering a setback. But you also have to push yourself a little harder each day to keep getting better. You have to determine this balance for yourself. Part of this means learning to say "No."

When should I say "No" if people are pushing me too hard?

Saying "no" is a difficult thing to do. Just the fact that you have this illness can make your self-confidence go way down. The social stigma associated with this illness is enough to get anyone feeling a little depressed. You want to please people and make them like you, so you want to agree to do what they say you should do. If you want to get better you have to stop worrying about what people think and start caring about what you yourself are able do. Take your medication on time and take care of yourself.

How often does your illness limit what you can do?

When I have spent a few hours working and my husband wants to go to the store, I have to tell him I can't go. He says that I am always saying "I'm too tired." If I let him convince me to do more in a day than I know I am able I will not be able to function as well the next day. If I go ahead and go to the store when I'm too tired we have a horrible time and probably will have a fight. It's better not to go. When I push myself way too far and get very tired, I sometimes even have hallucinations in the evening. Take it easy. You don't want to suffer a setback.

What else can make me feel better?

- Sunlight
Don't stay in your house all day watching TV. You need to be with other people. Get out in the sunlight every day for at least fifteen minutes. You need to get enough sunlight to prevent problems with seasonal affective disorder.[10] Not getting enough light can make you feel more depressed.

- Pets
If you like pets and are able to take care of them, cats and

dogs can make you feel a lot better. They don't judge you, listen to whatever you want to tell them, and are there for you whenever you need them. I have a wonderful Cocker Spaniel named Star who stays with me when I don't feel well. Just having her there makes me feel a lot better.

- Weight Control

Antipsychotic drugs can make people gain weight. They make you feel hungry. Weight gain is a terrible problem for people with schizoaffective disorder. It causes other physical problems like problems with your heart and diabetes. Weight gain can make you very depressed. Weight gain is something I struggle with every day.

- Candles and Scents

There is something else my counselor suggested that can make you feel better. Scented candles and air fresheners can have a comforting smell and are not too expensive. For some reason pleasant smells can make you feel better. I have no idea why it works but for some people it does. It won't cost too much to find out whether this helps you.

- Getting Enough Sleep

Sleeping well is one of the most important ways you can feel better. Make your bedroom feel safe and secure. Put up dark drapes if you feel more comfortable in the dark. If light makes you feel better, let the sun in your windows. Make sure you have a comfortable bed to sleep in. Naps can make it more difficult to have a good night's sleep. Try to stay awake in the daytime. Don't drink any drinks that contain caffeine after two p.m. If you don't sleep well, you are not going to feel well. Make your bedroom feel very safe for you. For some it's total darkness. For some it's a parakeet or a goldfish bowl. Make the room feel safe and secure for you.

- Taking Your Medication on Time

If you have problems remembering when to take your

medication, get a pill planner. Some people call it a med planner. You can buy one at a drugstore. They are plastic and have compartments for each day of the week. These planners help you remember what medication you need to take and whether you have already taken your medication that day.

CHAPTER FOUR
SUBSTANCE ABUSE

What happens if you have schizoaffective disorder and abuse drugs or alcohol?

Life with mental illness and a substance abuse problem is a special kind of hell I hope you never have to go through. I developed a substance abuse problem years after I was diagnosed with mental illness because I was stupid and drunk at a party and decided, "Why not?" Alcohol impairs your judgment. It only takes one time for a lot of illegal drugs to get you hooked.

A lot of people who are mentally ill drink and use drugs to try to make themselves feel better. They call this "self-medication." And the drugs and alcohol do make you feel better—at first. Then come the consequences. As Alcoholics Anonymous will tell you, if you don't stop, you're going to end up in jail, institutionalized, or dead.

What happens to people with substance abuse problems?

Be honest: Have you ever known an alcoholic or drug addict who kept using and ended up in a good situation? Who had a long and happy life? No. You see them gradually lose jobs, possessions, self-respect, and their families. They end up in jail from driving under the influence or drug possession. They can drive drunk and kill themselves and other people. Some even turn to prostitution or theft to support their habits. They contract AIDS and Hepatitis C. They damage their livers to the point of dying of cirrhosis.

If they use glass pipes and the end of the pipe breaks they can easily get AIDS. No one goes out to get a new pipe while they still have drugs to abuse. If you use the broken pipe with other people and the glass cuts their mouth, you could get AIDS or Hepatitis C from their blood on the pipe. Sharing needles and unprotected sex can cause the same problem. Do you really want AIDS or Hepatitis C? They are a guarantee of long, painful deaths.

Too much casual sex is a problem for people who are manic. You have the risk for sleeping with a lot of people during a manic phase[11]. Drugs can make you not care who you sleep with. If you are on drugs or drunk, you may not care whether you use a condom. AIDS is a definite possibility with multiple sexual partners. Do you really want to check out of your life this way?

I don't have that much of a problem. What are you talking about?

Have you been waiting to accept you have a problem until things get really bad? If the symptoms of your substance abuse problem are bad enough that your doctor is diagnosing a mental illness, the time is now. Things are really bad. It's time to quit using.

How do I know whether I have a substance abuse problem?

If you have to ask yourself that question at all it's a pretty good indication you have a substance abuse problem. If you are diagnosed with mental illness, that can also be a good indication you have a substance abuse problem. Your chances are about one in five that you do have this problem[12]. Substance abuse combined with mental illness is often called "dual diagnosis" or "double trouble." There are rehab centers which specialize in dual diagnosis.

Why do the mentally ill have more problems with substance abuse?

The simple answer is that people with serious mental illness (especially when the illness is untreated) don't feel very well. The drugs and alcohol make them feel better--at first. Doctors call this "self-medication."

How does my substance abuse problem affect my mental illness?

It will make your symptoms worse. It stops your medications from helping you feel better. Your psychiatric medications don't work when your are drinking or using drugs[13].

Is my problem bad enough that I need to get help?

The easiest way to answer that question is to try and stop on your own. If you can't stop on your own (and you probably won't be able to) then you need to get help. Chapter Twelve is about how I stopped using illegal substances.

CHAPTER FIVE
SOCIAL STIGMA

What is social stigma?

It's when people hold you in disgrace or reproach because you are mentally ill. It's not just for the mentally ill. It could be because of your race, your sexual orientation, or your handicap. It's why some people dislike you just because you're mentally ill or blame you for your illness.

Why do people seem to have a problem with the mentally ill?

People have attitudes about mental illness, ranging from acceptance to ignorance to fear to just plain meanness. This is not entirely their fault. Most of the time you hear about serious mental illness in the news or on television it is for one of two reasons: a) someone who is mentally ill has committed a crime or b) someone who has committed a crime is using a claim of mental illness to excuse their crime.

As I write this, people are talking about the Virginia Tech school shooting, the largest school shooting in the United State's history. The shooter was mentally ill but never received treatment. It is possible his family knew there was a problem but did not get help because they were embarrassed for people to know someone in their family had a mental problem. The shooting made people in my group therapy afraid that people would think even less of them.

You do not hear about the thousands of people who have schizoaffective disorder or other mental disorders who are just living their lives day to day. There is nothing to be ashamed about if you are mentally ill. It's not a choice you made. I know a lot of people who treat me like this illness is my own fault. Some have even treated me like this illness occurred because of sins I committed. They don't see mental illness as a physical problem of the brain. They are wrong. There is more about this in Chapter Eight.

Should I tell people I am mentally ill?

I don't care who knows anymore. I used to worry about it a lot. People aren't ever going to get rid of their misconceptions unless they have personal experience with someone who is not ashamed about being mentally ill. You don't have to tell anyone. My solution is just not to worry about it. You just have to ignore people who have bad attitudes about the mentally ill and go on with your life. It's doubtful you can change their minds--except slowly, through how they see you live your life.

How do you deal with ignorance about mental illness?

Ignore it as much as you can. But other people's ignorance will affect your life in many ways. People who distrust and do not understand mental illness do not vote to support the government programs that pay for your treatment. With some exceptions, politicians tend not to fight very hard for a group of people who people are afraid of, are too disabled to work, don't pay federal taxes, don't vote, and don't have much of a voice in our society.

Stigma bothers a lot of people in group therapy with me and they talk about it a lot. I belong to some internet online schizoaffective groups and people discuss being "outed" at work and the problems it causes them. In the end, you just have to decide which people you should let know about your illness and which ones won't be able to handle knowing about the problem.

CHAPTER SIX
PRESCRIPTION DRUGS

If I feel better, can I stop taking my medication?

The biggest mistake people with schizoaffective disorder make is to stop taking their medication because they feel better. Stopping your medications all at once is a very good way to end up in the hospital. If you are feeling better, it is probably because the medication is working. Never stop taking any psychiatric medication until you talk to your doctor.

It's driving me crazy to wait to take my next dose. Should I take my medication early?

Don't give in and take your medication early. If you are having a hard time waiting, tell your doctor as soon as you can. It may be that your dosage is not high enough.

I'm having terrible symptoms. Why can't I take my medication early?

As bad as you feel right now, you are going to feel worse when it's time to take your next dose and it's not there because you already took it. The doctor and clinic are not going to give you extra medication just because you took yours early. Taking your medication early means you are going to run out before it's time to refill your prescription. Don't give in and take it early. It's much better to wait than to run out of pills later.

I'm out of my medication and I can't get a refill until tomorrow. What should I do?

Call your doctor or clinic and try to get the refill today. Sometimes this may not work. For instance, it's Monday and it's Memorial Day and the offices and pharmacies are closed. If I have to go through a night without medication, this is what I do.

What do you do when you run out of medication and can't sleep?

I admit to myself that I'm probably not going to be able to sleep. Not sleeping makes me feel terrible. I tell myself I just have to get through that night and that I can get my medication in the morning. I try taking a hot bath or shower to relax my muscles and help me get to sleep. I go to bed and try to sleep. If I start to lie there not sleeping and worrying more and more that I'm not going to sleep, I get out of bed.

Lying in bed worrying is not going to help anything. I do something to relax me until morning. I either read a book that usually puts me to sleep (think *Moby Dick*) or I read some of the Old Testament which relaxes me. If you ever go to sleep watching a movie you think is boring, buy a copy of it to use when you can't sleep. Try watching infomercials or something on TV that is really boring.

I make necklaces out of beads all night which really calms me down. Do whatever works for you. Tell yourself, "I'm out of medication again, I've been through this before, I'll make it until morning, then I'll get my refills and sleep. I've done it before and I can do it again." In the morning, when your clinic or doctor's office opens, be sure to get help.

I recently was diagnosed with schizoaffective disorder. Which medication will I need to take?

It may take a lot of tries to find the medications that will help you the best. The medication you are prescribed may help you right away. Or it may take some time to find the medication that will help you. Some medications take a couple of weeks or even a month to build up enough in your body to work. Just be prepared to be patient. Keep on trying and you and your doctor will find the right ones. It may take a long time, but now you know your diagnosis and your doctor will find the medication that's right for you.

What types of medication might the doctor prescribe for me?

The types of medication your doctor may prescribe are: 1) anti-psychotics for hallucinations, delusions, and paranoia, 2) a mood stabilizer for mania and depression, 3) possibly an anti-depressant, 4) something to help you sleep, and (if you really need it), 5) something to help you relax.

Each new medication you take may or may not work for you. Different medicines work for different people. For example, Wellbutrin (an anti-depressant) works well for many people. It causes side effects for me and does not lift my depression at all. Effexor (another anti-depressant) works very well for me and does not cause side effects. This does not mean that Wellbutrin won't work for you and it does not mean that Effexor will work for you. Medication that works for me may not work for you at all. You need to give them a try as your doctor prescribes them and be patient.

How do I know which medication will work for me?

Trial and error. There is medication out there that can help you. It just may take time to know what that medication will be. You are going to have to be ready to wait to find the right medication. You may not feel very well while you are waiting for the medication to work. Be proud you are taking responsibility for helping yourself. You are on your way to feeling better.

Each new medication you try may or may not work and it may cause side effects. No doctor can predict which side effects a medication may cause. They are different for every person who takes the drug. Side effects for me from different medications have included bed wetting, muscle spasms, inability to control the muscles in the face, tight muscles that make it difficult to walk normally, weight gain, and many others. Weird symptoms like this happened to me one at a time when I tried a new medication (not all at once). You may not have any side effects at all. But each time I had a bad side effect I had to try another medication and be patient again to see if it would work.

I am now taking medication that helps me very well and I am not experiencing any side effects other than weight gain. You will find medications that help you. You can't just take some medication and expect to feel better overnight. But you can feel better and better every day as you learn to manage your illness on your own and the medication starts to work.

CHAPTER SEVEN
HANDLING PROBLEMS
WITH PSYCHIATRISTS

How do you find a good psychiatrist?

I have seen some wonderful understanding psychiatrists over the years. Most of the time I have been ill I have lived in large cities. I was seen by many good doctors during those times. If you are lucky enough to be able to pay to see a psychiatrist or you have good insurance, the best way to find a good psychiatrist is word of mouth.

I am so ill I can't work. What if I can't pay to see a psychiatrist?

I am on Social Security disability like many people who are unable to work at a regular full time job. If you can't afford a private psychiatrist and pay for your own medication you have to go to a government-funded clinic. This is a problem because psychiatrists don't stay very long at clinics that people on Medicare or Medicaid can afford. This means you won't see any one psychiatrist for very long.

I have encountered a lot of doctors who work with the mentally ill out of compassion and not concern about their salary. But most of the doctors who are working at these clinics are there sometimes because they are unable to get a job anywhere else. Dissatisfied with the poor working conditions and low pay, medical professionals go through clinics in small towns as if the clinics had revolving doors. They may leave before they have even seen you enough times to count on the fingers of one hand.

Why is switching doctors a problem?

Each new doctor has little time to familiarize themselves with the complicated medical records of someone with a history of mental illness. This can mean your medications are either changed too frequently or not enough. This can happen even after you have spent months achieving the right balance of medication to make you feel better. You can tell the doctor you are feeling fine and don't want to change, but some doctors will change your medication anyway.

If you are having problems with your medication a new doctor may not want to change your medication the first time they see you. And by your next appointment you might see a new doctor again.

If you are doing fine on your current medications resist strongly when a new doctor wants to change them. Don't be afraid to tell the doctor you do not want your medication changed. It is not going to hurt anything to tell them what you want.

My medications are working fine and a new doctor is changing my prescription. Why?

Doctors like to prescribe medicines that have worked well for their other patients in the past. Each new doctor seems to have their own favorite drugs they prescribe. It may have taken months for you to find the medication that helps you. The new doctor may want to change your medications anyway. This is extremely frustrating.

I get nervous when I see a new doctor. It can be hard for me to stand up to a new doctor and ask firmly to stay on the same medication. I ask my counselor to come into the meeting the first time I see a new doctor to help me tell the doctor that my medication is already helping me.

What happens if my medication gets changed?

The new drug a doctor suggests to you may work very well with no side effects. But each time your prescription is changed is a risk. Psychiatric drugs can have terrible side effects. Muscle twitching, drooling, eyes rolling in the back of your head, muscles so tight you have trouble walking, weight gain--and the list goes on. There are even lawsuits about prescription drugs that have given people diabetes and other serious problems such as birth defects.

Learning to calmly wait during a medication change is part of the recovery process for schizoaffective disorder. Each psychiatric drug works differently for different people. The outcome of a change in medication could be one of three things: the drug works well for you with no side effects, the drug does not work for you, or the drug does not work and you still experience side effects. The dosage of the new drug may need to be increased over time in order for it to work at all. It is going to take time to straighten things out. Maybe the most important thing about schizoaffective disorder is learning patience.

If the clinic you go to switches doctors a lot and a doctor changes your medication, he or she may not even be there on your next visit. Then you may have another new doctor and a new problem with your medication. Some doctors will even change your diagnosis. In the end what the doctor says goes (at least for that visit). After all, he or she is the doctor.

Should I take the new medication the doctor prescribes for me?

You may not have any choice. If you can't pay for a private doctor and you can't afford the medication any other way than through the government clinic, you have to take the new medication as prescribed. You won't know whether it will work. You won't know what side effects you may experience. You have to accept that your medications are going to switch from time to time if you can't afford to see a private physician. And the new medication may work out just fine.

What if my new medication does not help me?

If the new medication doesn't work for you, ask for your medication to be switched back to your old prescription at your next office visit. Be sure to keep track of exactly which medications were working for you and write down the dosage you were on. You can ask your counselor to help you with this. In the meantime, give the new medication a chance to work. New medications may need to be taken for several weeks to build up in your system before they work.

You may want to take it easy if you suffer withdrawal from the old medication. I tell myself, "You're in that situation again, you're not feeling so well, they're changing your meds again, just wait and see what happens, don't get upset, the new medication may work out." And sometimes it does. Sometimes you can end up hospitalized if your medication isn't helping you.

What if the area I live in does not have a psychiatric hospital?

There is also a problem with getting taken to a good psychiatric hospital if you ever need to be hospitalized. The hospitals with psychiatric facilities are in large cities and you need a way to get there. The local ambulance service is probably not going to drive you to a large city to take you to a psychiatric facility. You may have to find your own transportation.

CHAPTER EIGHT
OMEGA-3 SUPPLEMENTS

What supplements should I take to help with my symptoms?

Doctors are beginning to recommend omega-3 fatty acid supplements as a treatment for several mental illnesses.[14] Omega-3 fatty acids (found in fish oil, flaxseed oil) have been shown to reduce schizophrenia, depression, bipolar disorder, and ADHD symptoms.[15] Because schizoaffective disorder is a combination of schizophrenic and bipolar symptoms, it stands to reason that omega-3 will work for people with schizoaffective disorder.

People with depression and schizophrenia have reduced levels of omega-3 fatty acids in their red blood cells.[16] People who did not respond to psychiatric treatment for depression and schizophrenia felt better when they added omega-3 fatty acids to their diet. Even people already taking psychotropic medications (drugs that affect brain function) reported feeling better when they took omega-3 fatty acid supplements. So don't stop taking your medications! If you want to try omega-3 supplements take your regular medication also.

The two main fatty acids in omega-3 are EPA and DHA. EPA affects nerve call activity. The best results happened when people took at least 2000 mg of EPA per day (but not more).[17] The omega-3 supplement you buy will list the amount of EPA it contains. This will mean taking several fish oil pills to get the suggested 2000 mg EPA.

Important Warning: The previous chapter is provided for information purposes only. It covers possible complementary treatment approaches that may be used in concert with antipsychotic medications. The adoption of any of these complementary treatments should be done with a qualified psychiatrist or psychologist's knowledge and approval as part of a person's complete treatment plan. This summary of possible complementary treatments is for informational purposes only.

CHAPTER NINE
COUNSELORS

Why do I need a counselor? I already see a doctor.

Your counselor can be your best ally to help you get better. You may not always know if you are having a setback. Someone needs to see you regularly who can recognize whether you are having problems. Even a deterioration in personal cleanliness and not sleeping can be indications.

You may not be aware you are having hallucinations or delusions and you may not be the first to know you are manic or depressed. Family members and friends who see you all the time may know something is wrong but may not be able to tell what it is. Your counselor is trained to recognize these problems.

What if I don't like my counselor? What if we don't get along?

I went through a few counselors who couldn't put up with me before I finally found the counselor I have now. I don't blame any of them. I can be very hard to deal with when I am not feeling well.

The counselor I have now I have seen for years. She is the best one I have ever had. She has helped me by teaching me about this illness and has made many suggestions about how to feel better. She has taken the time to see me whenever I need her. She and the director of the clinic have come down to the emergency room in the past few years to help me many times. The doctors came and went, but she has been there consistently.

In order to feel better you need to find the best counselor you can. If you are lucky, you will also find a very good friend.

CHAPTER TEN
GROUP THERAPY

Should I go to group therapy?

If you want your life to change so you can feel better you need to get out and talk to people with the same or similar illnesses. You need to make friends and get outside your house. Staying in your house all day by yourself is not going to make you feel better.

I'm so sick I can hardly leave the house. What should I do?

If you feel you are not well enough to go out and be around people, just try to get a little stronger every day. Start by calling people you know on the phone. Call your counselor and let him/her know you are having trouble getting out of the house. Go to the store. Go to the library. Go to group therapy. Just don't stay at home by yourself. (Don't go anywhere they serve alcohol.)

What is it like going to group therapy?

I go to a group that was started by my clinic. We meet once a week. It's a group for mental health consumers at the clinic and it is led by another mental health consumer. They call us consumers here, not patients. The group is not run by the clinic but by the mental health consumers themselves.

The lady who chairs our group is very nice. She is doing so well she no longer has to go to my clinic. She just gets her medication from her regular physician. But she did not stop leading the group. She cares about us all too much.

We have one member with multiple personality disorder, a few with bipolar disorder, and some people with schizophrenia and schizoaffective disorder. When I first started going to the group I just listened but didn't talk. I have seen several people who joined the group after I did who didn't say anything for a while until they got more comfortable being in the group. They kept coming back and that's what is important.

Do the people in the group ever upset you?

Sometimes the things that people talk about in group can make you uncomfortable. A very good friend of mine in the group was abused sexually by her parents as young as three years old. She now has children and she doesn't have custody. She has bipolar disorder, a drinking problem, a boyfriend who encourages her to drink and spends his whole paycheck on beer. I talk to her whenever I can. Alcohol was keeping her medication from helping her. Alcohol plus the medication she was taking made her sleep most of the time.

A few weeks ago she came to the group and talked and talked about her problems with alcohol and how unhappy she was. It was difficult to listen to. I've known her for years and this was the first time I have ever heard her asking for help. She was asking for help and crying and I know this outburst was difficult for a lot of the group members to hear.

Still, she needed us and we needed her. It helps a lot to know that there are others out there with problems that are similar to yours.

Now, a few weeks later, she is getting help. She left town yesterday to be in a group home where there's no alcoholic boyfriend and the staff there can help her remember when to take her medication. I believe her counselor and being in our group helped her take these steps toward feeling better.

What if I'm in group and something makes me uncomfortable?

You can either tell people you're uncomfortable or just leave the meeting for a few minutes for a break. We now have an agreement in our group that if we are uncomfortable with any subject or anything that is happening it's OK for us to tell each other. We went through a lot together before we made this agreement.

Will everything I say at group therapy be confidential?

My group has an agreement that anything we say during the group is confidential. But over the years we have been together we have made an exception. When you're worried someone in the group might hurt themselves or someone has stopped taking their medication it is OK for us to tell their counselor or someone else who can help them. We made the exception because the way some people acted in group made us afraid for them. It was too difficult to keep what they said confidential if we were worried they might be in real trouble.

The group you go to may have different rules. The rules in our group have developed over the years we have been meeting. We have gotten more and more comfortable with each other as time has gone by. You can see the group is helping people as they get better and better.

How did going to group help you?

The group leader is someone I know I can count on if I'm not feeling well. I can call her if I have a problem and she is a really good listener. If it weren't for her and the director of the adult activity center where I spend my mornings, this book would never have been written. The therapy group is held at this center.

I'm not sure the people at the center knew what to think about the mental health group meeting at first. Now everyone there is used to it. They have a computer room that's free for the public to use. I didn't have a computer at home, but I love the internet and I wanted to write this book. I started going up there every day and staying a few hours.

The more I got out of the house, the better I felt. I made friends up there. It changed my life. This center was originally designed for senior citizens who weren't feeling well so that they would have someplace to go and be with people and feel better. After a time they realized younger adults needed a place to go also. Now the center is for all adults. Try to find someplace to like this to go to every day and get out of the house. Large cities may even have a clubhouse for the mentally ill.

Trying to get better and getting out of the house will put you in touch with people and places you never imagined were there. The more you try to make yourself better by being around other people the better your life will be. Before I started going to group and my counselor asked me what my goals were I said to maintain things the way they were and not get any sicker. Now I have dreams of doing things I never thought could have been possible. It's because of my counselor, our group leader, and the activity center.

CHAPTER ELEVEN
THE HOSPITAL

Me—in the hospital?

The hospital is nothing to be afraid of. It's just another tool you can use to help you get better if you are really having problems. There are several reasons you might need to be hospitalized at some point (if you haven't been already). If you have bipolar disorder, schizophrenia, or schizoaffective disorder there is a good chance you'll end up in the hospital a few times. This doesn't mean that *you* will ever have to go. You are an individual and not a statistic. But even if you have never been to the hospital before, this illness means you are just not emotionally as strong as "normal" people. The death of a loved one or another stressful event could be more than you could handle. Because of your illness, you have a greater chance of being hospitalized so you need to plan ahead. If you don't plan ahead you could end up in a very bad situation.

Is a psychiatric facility a scary place?

Don't let going to the hospital scare you. It's a good place to be if you need a major medication adjustment, the illness just gets to be more than you can handle, there is too much stress in your life, you are thinking of suicide, or you are having bad side effects from your medication.

OK, I'm having too many problems to handle. What do I do now?

If you feel that you need to go to the emergency room, of course you can call 911 on your own or have someone drive you there. But sometimes people with bipolar disorder, schizophrenia, and schizoaffective disorder can do things that seem very abnormal because they have hallucinations and delusions. I carry a letter with me which contains my diagnosis, my doctor's name, and emergency contact information. You can ask your counselor for a letter like this to carry with you.

If someone gets frightened by your behavior, they may call an ambulance because they feel you might be dangerous to yourself or others. It can help a lot if you have a letter which explains your illness and lets people know who to contact if you are having problems. You may not be able to explain it very well yourself at the time.

I called the ambulance, but what are those policemen doing here? Are they going to arrest me?

If someone calls an ambulance for you or if you call because you are concerned about yourself, an ambulance may be sent, but be aware that the police will probably come also. Don't let the fact that the police are there scare you. They are there to protect you and the paramedics who are responding to the call. Don't be paranoid and afraid that the police are there to arrest you.

It is a routine thing for the police to be there. The police will probably follow the ambulance to the hospital and stay with you until you have been seen and released or admitted to the hospital. Most cities have police who are specially trained to help those with mental illnesses. It's probably not the first time the police have been out on a call like this. They are just there to make sure you get help and that you don't hurt yourself or anyone else.

I changed my mind—can I go home now?

If you have attempted or threatened to hurt yourself, you have probably lost the option to change your mind and stay home. The reason for this is liability. If the paramedics do not take you to the hospital and you hurt yourself or someone else, they are facing a lawsuit. So once they are there and they want to take you to the emergency room you are going to have to go. The more you cooperate, the better off you are going to be. The more rational and cooperative you can be, the sooner you are going to be released from the hospital so you can go home.

Can they make me go get help, even if I don't want to?

Yes. If they believe you are a danger to yourself or others they can force you to go to a state facility in handcuffs if you don't cooperate. If you refuse to go with them and get help, they can force you to go through the civil commitment process. This means you are forcing them to fill out a lot of paperwork, wake up a judge, and get you committed to a psychiatric facility. They are not going to be thrilled about having to do this just because you won't cooperate. If your goal is to get out of the hospital as soon as you can, a civil commitment to a state facility is not what you want.

Why don't I want to go to a state facility?

Go voluntarily to a private facility if you can. Private facilities are usually much, much nicer than state facilities. They have more funding and can provide a better place for you to get well. In Texas, the state psychiatric facility in is on the same grounds and has the same common area as the facility for the criminally insane. These patients were found to be incompetent to stand trial or were found not guilty by reason of insanity. The state then determines whether or not these patients are "manifestly dangerous" and then puts them in the state facility with you and other non-violent people who are mentally ill. So go to a private hospital if you can.

What private hospital should I go to?

Private hospitals are a lot nicer than state facilities, but they are not all the same. Some overmedicate you to keep you quiet and manageable until they release you and file the insurance claim. Others have a wonderful staff, nurses, psychiatrists and group sessions that can really help you. Ask your doctor, counselor, or even members of your group therapy sessions what hospital they recommend. That way you can tell the paramedics the name of the hospital to which you would like to be taken. You can even ask your counselor to put the name of the hospital you prefer on the letter explaining your condition. You need to know which hospital is best before you get in a situation like this, so don't wait--find out today.

Will they let me smoke in the hospital?

Maybe. If you smoke, be aware that some hospitals don't allow you to smoke. If you do end up in a hospital where you can't smoke, ask your doctor for a patch. It can keep you from going through withdrawal from cigarettes on top of whatever else it is that got you into the hospital in the first place. If they will let you smoke, you are going to need to furnish your own cigarettes. The hospital staff is not going to buy them for you.

What kind of clothes can I wear in the hospital?

You can't wear shoelaces, revealing clothing, or underwire bras. You can't bring any glass, like a make-up mirror, into the hospital. Remember to bring warm clothing and socks. The hospitals can keep the temperature very low.

Will I still have a place to live when I get out of the hospital?

If you are hospitalized for any length of time, it can be a lifesaver to have someone you trust who can pay your rent and bills while you are away. My husband does this for me, but if I weren't married, I would give my parents or someone I really trusted the ability to pay my bills while I was gone. If you don't have anyone who can do this for you, some banks can pay your bills for a fee.

Don't wait too late to set this up. If you have a serious mental illness there is a pretty good chance you are going to the hospital at some point during your life. Be ready for it. Once I did not have someone to pay my bills while I was gone and I got out of the hospital with no place to live and a bill from the apartment complex for selling my furniture in my absence. While you are in the hospital you have enough to worry about without wondering if you will be homeless and without a phone and electricity when you get out. Plan ahead.

What happens in the emergency room?

When you get to the emergency room you can expect to wait a very long time to be admitted to the psychiatric ward or to be released. The one exception is when you try to hurt yourself by taking something (and then you get to have your stomach pumped right away)! Believe me, this is not an enjoyable experience.

It's just fact of life that the emergency room can take a long time. Try not to get upset, just try to relax and wait. You may be hurting a lot emotionally, but as long as the emergency room staff considers you stable people in the emergency room with broken arms or other physical problems are going to be seen first.

I finally got to the psychiatric ward. What now?

Once you are admitted to a psychiatric ward, you're probably going to be exhausted just from the process of getting to the ward through the emergency room. Take a day and sleep. But as soon as you can, if you want to be released from the hospital, you need to participate in group therapy, talk and get along with the other patients, and act like a normal human being. If you stay in your room all the time it is going to take you a lot longer to get out of the hospital.

What's it like being in a locked ward?

It can get claustrophobic. Not going outside in the sun for a couple of weeks can be very depressing. But if you are having a hard time and need to be in the hospital, a locked ward can make you feel safe. You know that a lot of visitors and other people will not be wandering around the ward. A steady routine and seeing the same people all the time can be comforting.

Why are the other patients acting that way?

Remember, they are there because they are very sick. Very rarely, patients will make racial slurs, call people bad names, attempt to cause fights, or be very loud. The security staff on the ward will make sure you are in a safe environment.

If someone is causing a lot of problems on the ward they will be medicated or confined to another area. If someone is causing you a lot of trouble, just stay away from them. Stay in your room until they calm down or tell a nurse or tech about the problem.

One girl I will always remember was making a lot of racial comments and upsetting a lot of people. She was given some medicine and she calmed down. I started talking to her about why she had been hospitalized. She told me that when she was thirteen, her fifteen-year-old brother had sexually abused her. She became pregnant and her parents raised her daughter as if her daughter was her sister. Her brother was still allowed in the house and her daughter/sister was getting old enough that she was afraid he would molest her. And I thought I had problems!

So just remember: people that are acting up in a mental ward—you have no idea what they have been through. Don't pick a fight. Just go to your room for a while until they calm down.

I don't like it here. I want to leave right now. What do I do?

Relax and calm down. That's the best way to get discharged from the hospital. But people who really want to get out of the hospital quickly sometimes sign out AMA (against medical advice). This is not a good idea. Usually your smoking privileges are taken away immediately. You will be forcing the hospital staff to fill out a lot of forms and they also must have you seen by a doctor within a short period of time to assess whether you are a danger to yourself or others. If you are released, you will not be given a prescription for medication. You will not be given any prescription drugs to take with you. You will be on your own. So calm down and wait to be discharged when you are really ready.

I'm finally getting discharged. What do I need to do before I leave?

The hospital is not going to give you medication to take with you. Make very sure you read the prescription your doctor wrote and make sure it is correct—both the medicines and the dosages. Mistakes are made in prescribing medicine all the time. Once you are released from the hospital you will have a very hard time getting your prescription corrected.

Make sure you have a way to fill your prescriptions so you won't run out. If you run out of medication, you will probably just end up back in the hospital. Next, think about what day of the week it is. If you get your medication from a clinic and they are closed on Saturday and Sunday, don't let the hospital release you on Friday afternoon. Wait in the hospital until the next Monday morning, when you can get your medication. Spending the weekend with no medication is a terrible idea for someone who just got out of the hospital.

If you get your medication from a clinic, have the hospital fax the clinic your prescriptions and your discharge information before you leave the hospital. Once you are out of the hospital it's going to be a lot harder to get the staff to fax this information. This is not because they don't care about you once you leave, it's just that they have people right there in front of them who have problems and the people who are right in front of them are going to get helped before someone calling on the phone.

Call the clinic or place you receive your medicine *yourself* and ask them if they have all the paperwork they need before you leave the hospital. Don't just let the hospital staff tell you it has been sent. Make sure yourself.

Take a copy of your discharge papers and your prescriptions with you. Make sure you know the number to the nurse's station at the hospital before you leave in case there are any unexpected problems.

Now I'm out of the hospital and I don't feel well. Why?

A lot of stress from day-to-day life goes away when you go to the hospital. Routines and schedules control every part of your hospitalization. When you get home, you have to cook, shop for groceries, clean your house, wash your clothes, go to doctor's appointments, answer the phone, interact with friends and relatives, and deal with everyday stress. Since you have been living in a safe, closed environment, the adjustment when you get back home can be difficult. It helps me to rest as much as I can. Even if you feel fine when you leave the hospital you may feel a little worse at home right after you are released. Just expect a readjustment period when you get home.

I was fine in the hospital, but now that I'm home I'm starting to have side effects from my new medications. What do I do?

A lot of psychiatric medicine slowly build up in your body each day you take a new dose. This can mean side effects can take a while to appear. If you get home and start experiencing side effects, call your counselor or doctor and let someone know. Some side effects can be dangerous. It is important to follow up on this.

CHAPTER TWELVE
RELIGION

Should I go to church?

I think it is a very good idea to go to church. Fellow church members can be a very good support system for you and socializing with as many people as you can will make you feel better.

What church should I attend?

I would not presume to tell you which church to attend. But I do want to tell you about a problem I experienced at a local church.

People at church can have an quite an attitude about mental illness and even illness in general. Some believe that most illness is caused by sin. They do not seem to believe that mental illness actually exists. They believe it is a problem caused by sin and the influence of demons or the devil.

What if the people at my church tell me I don't need my medication?

Not only may they point at mental illness as a result of sin, but they may also encourage you to stop taking your medication. There was a distrust at a church I went to of psychologists and psychiatrists in general. In the Bible, Mark 5 is an account about someone who appears to me to have suffered from severe mental illness. This man was plagued by demons and Jesus drove them out of him. At the end of the chapter, the man is seated comfortably and dressed normally asking to accompany Jesus on his mission.

People can use this chapter and other examples in the Bible to suggest that mental illness can be cured by faith and prayer. They would not tell a diabetic to pray and stop using insulin. They would not tell someone with cancer to stop chemotherapy. But they may tell you that you do not need psychiatric medication because they don't understand that mental illness is a real chronic illness of the body that requires treatment.

If you are diagnosed with schizoaffective disorder it is not because you are possessed by demons. It is not because you committed a sin. It is not because of a lack of faith. Your brain is physically different from "normal" people. If you are taking psychiatric medications do not stop taking them without talking to your doctor. If you do stop taking your medication and you get worse, Jesus' ability to heal will not be questioned. Instead, your lack of adequate faith will be found to be the cause. And you will be blamed once again for causing your own illness.

I am reminded of a joke I heard. A man is sitting on the roof of his house surrounded by a flood. A boat comes by and offers to carry him to safety. He refuses saying that God will save him. Another boat comes by and he refuses help a second time. The floods rise and he drowns. At the pearly gates he asks God why he didn't save him. God replies, "I sent you two boats!"

Your medication and your psychiatrist are the boats God

has sent you to help make you well. In New Testament times, these medications had not been invented. Stay on your medications and get the help you need. It was even suggested that I was a drug addict for taking the medication that was prescribed for me. If people try to get you to stop taking your medications and heal yourself by faith, find another church. Quickly.

What other groups should I avoid?

Any groups or anyone who tells you not to take your medication. Stay away from the "church" of Scientology. They hate psychiatry and psychiatric medications. There are other groups out there who will try to tell you that you don't need your medication. Just steer clear of them.

CHAPTER THIRTEEN
HOW I STOPPED MY SUBSTANCE ABUSE

How do I get help for a substance abuse problem?

I can only tell you what I did to get better. All the things I did may not work for you. There are inpatient and outpatient facilities that can help. I did not go to one of these but it doesn't mean you shouldn't. Alcoholics Anonymous (AA) and Cocaine Anonymous (CA) did not work for me, but that does not mean you shouldn't try them.

The problem I had over the years with AA and CA is that the people in the group have substance abuse problems. When you are quitting, I do not believe that you should be around anyone else who has a substance abuse problem. If you attend AA or CA, do not go anywhere other than the meeting with anyone who has less than several years of sobriety.

Any time you are around anyone who doesn't have several years sobriety outside the meeting your chance of slipping up increases. You may be tempted to use each other as an excuse to drink or use drugs. If the person you are with has a problem with substance abuse, it is entirely possible that one of you might suggest that "A beer sounds really good right now." So you can use each other's weaknesses to support the idea that it's really OK to use alcohol or drugs "just this one time." This is why you're going to have to stay away from anyone you know you have ever used with. I mean staying away from them entirely.

If my friends and/or family use, can I see them?

Not right now. You are going to have to completely change your life until you are strong in your sobriety. When things get really bad I recommend leaving your current situation entirely. I just got up and left the city where I lived. The only apartment I could afford was in a Section 8 complex and it was full of crime, poverty, and drugs. I moved to a small town in Texas. I didn't know anyone who had a substance abuse problem in the new town. And if I meet someone like that I stay away from them.

There are a lot of people who use where I live. Where should I move?

Due to my problem with substance abuse and the desire to live in a nicer place, I moved to a small, rural area. Apartments here are a lot cheaper. Low rent housing in a large city is no fun. It means problem neighbors and being surrounded by drug use.

The city I live in is beautiful. Our apartment is quiet. There was one crime reported at our large apartment complex last year--one slashed tire. There is almost no traffic and no pollution. There are a whole lot more churches than bars in this city.

I picked this small town because my parents (who would never use drugs) live an hour's drive from this small town. But they didn't really want to see me or have anything to do with me because they were sick and tired of me using. I was past the point of being trusted, but I did ask them for help. They let me stay at a house on their land for a week so I wouldn't be homeless. They even bought us groceries. You may not have family that will help you. There is other help available.

Who should I count on while I am recovering?

The best people to be around when you are quitting are people who have never and never will have a problem with substance abuse. You cannot be around anyone you have ever used with or you are preparing yourself for failure. I mean just picking up everything you haven't pawned that you can carry and leaving the rest. Just get out of the bad situation and change everything. You are not going to get better by sticking around.

What if I don't have enough money to move?

Move anyway. I sold my car to have enough money to pay for somewhere else to live. I would bet you have been pretty creative about finding money to buy whatever substance you are abusing (if any). You can get enough money together to move. There is a hotel where I lived that has a furnished room with all bills and cable paid that is very inexpensive. It wasn't very fancy but it got me away from the people I knew who were using.

Who will help me change?

There are churches all over America who will help you stop using. I went to a local church and told them I was trying to quit. They bought me groceries until enough Social Security money came that I could buy them myself. Other churches gave me clothing and even a few books to read.

How do I make new friends?

Church is a good place to meet people who don't use drugs or alcohol. But there are plenty of people who go to church who do have substance abuse problems. Make sure you know what you are getting in to before you make new friends.

The MHMR center is not a good place to make new friends if you are trying to quit. This is because at least one in five of them do have substance abuse problems. Get to know people very well you meet at group therapy or in the lobby of the clinic or doctor's office before you see them socially. Make sure they don't have a problem before you get to know them really well or you are asking for more trouble.

The only time I have fun is when I am using. What would it be like not to use anymore?

If you're still having fun while you're using it won't last much longer. Soon it will be a cycle of getting high and trying to find some way to get money, pawning or stealing something else, doing God knows what to get more of the substance you are abusing. The longer you use, the more of a nightmare your life becomes. I felt like I was living in hell but it was just a hell of my own creation. Now I understand there are places and times on Earth that can seem a lot like heaven.

CHAPTER FOURTEEN
POVERTY, JAIL AND HOMELESSNESS

Why are so many of the mentally ill in jail or homeless?

A large percentage of the mentally ill live in poverty. They are too sick to work and must depend on Social Security. Social Security payments can be very low. If your payments are low you may qualify for reduced Section 8 housing. You may also qualify for food stamp programs. You can get by on Social Security, but it's not easy.

Some people with schizoaffective disorder aren't together enough to apply and qualify for benefits. Many are homeless.

Since the mentally ill are more likely to have substance abuse problems, they often end up in jail. If not for drug offenses, they are in jail for related offenses: theft or prostitution to get the substance to which they are addicted. They are also arrested for trespassing when they are homeless and try to find a place to stay. After they have been in jail they may end up homeless. So if you are addicted to anything, stop now and get your life together before you end up in jail or homeless.

CHAPTER FIFTEEN
MOVING FORWARD

I have written this book about probabilities. The probability you'll go to the hospital at some point. The possibility you may have or develop a problem with substance abuse. But you are one person. You are not a number. You don't have to experience these problems at all. You may have the same doctor for years and never experience the difficulties associated with changing doctors all the time.

If you know enough to recognize that these problems can occur when you least expect them, you can see these problems for what they are: temporary setbacks. Remember how to deal with them and you are way ahead of the game.

I know that all the things I have written about in this book will help me feel better. I'm not perfect. I don't do all of these things all the time. You can't change your life all at once. You have to start a little bit at a time. If you mess up, dust yourself off and start again.

You can have love and happiness in your life. Mental illness does not disqualify you. You can get rid of almost all of the hallucinations (if you even ever had them) and you can remember the good times to help you through the times you may be depressed. You can learn to ignore people who aren't so nice to you because you are ill. If you don't feel well you can be assured at some point in the near future you will feel a lot better. You have to take responsibility for helping yourself feel better because the steps you take to combat this illness truly affect how you feel. The movies *A Beautiful Mind* and *Shine* can change how you feel about the concept of recovery from mental illness.

This illness for me is a cycle of a lot of good times followed by periods of not doing so well. The hospital stays are shorter now. The problems are less difficult because I've been through them before. If you're new to schizoaffective disorder, just remember it's going to get easier and you may even feel better the older you are. It just takes some time. Be patient.

Mary Dodds lives in a small town in Texas. She practiced law in Houston, Texas, for a short while before she was diagnosed with mental illness. This book was written fourteen years later, after many hospitalizations, antipsychotics, antidepressants and mood stabilizer drugs. She has won a long and difficult battle with substance abuse. She is now working part-time writing and happily living with her husband, Mitch, and their dog, Star. The chapters in this book contain information and insight and are what she wishes someone had told her at the beginning of her battle with this illness.

ENDNOTES:

[1] The Louis de la Parte Florida Mental Health Institute, University of South Florida, "Mental Health Parity, National and State Perspectives: A REPORT" (March 1997)

[2] groups/yahoo.com

[3] E. Fuller Torrey, M.D. and Michael B. Knable., D.O., *Surviving Manic Depression* (Basic Books, 2002), p.116; Torrey, E. Fuller, M.D., *Surviving Schizophrenia* (Quill, 2001), p.143.

[4] Kay McCray, Ed. D., Director, Patient & Family Education, "Frequently Asked Questions (FAQs) about Schizoaffective Disorder," (G. Werber Bryan Psychiatric Hospital, Columbia, South Carolina, 1998), p.2.

[5] Christine Haran, "Substance Abuse Relapses: Could it Be a Dual Diagnosis?" (Healthology, 2004) p.1.

[6] Torrey & Knable, pp. 63-4.

[7] Id., p.98.

[8] McCray, p.1.

[9] Id.

[10] Torrey & Knable, pp. 99-100.

[11] Id., p. 98.

[12] McCray, p.2.

[13] Ricardo Castaneda, Marc Galanter, Harold Lifshuts & Hugo Franco, "Effect of Drug Abuse on Psychiatric Symptoms Among Hospitalized Schizophrenics" (American Journal of Drug and Alcohol Abuse, Sept. 1991).

[14] Peet M. Stokes, "Omega-3 fatty acids in the treatment of psychiatric disorders (1st Vitality.com, 2005),p.1051-9.

[15] Id., pp. 1051-9.

[16] Id.

[17] David F. Horrobin, "Omega-3 Fatty Acid for Schizophrenia" (Am J Psychiatry, January 2003), p.1.

CPSIA information can be obtained at www.ICGtesting.com
Printed in the USA
265828BV00003B/395/P